Whales, Dolphins & Porpoises

Naturally Scottish

Scottish Natural Heritage
Dualchas Nàdair na h-Alba
All of nature for all of Scotland
Nàdar air fad airson Alba air fad

Authors: Katie Gillham and John Baxter
Contributions from: Michael Scott, Lynne Farrell
Acknowledgements: Advice and comments from Caroline Weir,
Dominic Shann, staff at the National Poetry Library in Edinburgh
Series Editor: John Baxter (SNH)
Design and production: SNH Publishing

www.snh.org.uk

Photography: ANT Photo Library/NHPA 16; Janet Baxter 10 top, back cover; John Baxter opposite introduction top;
Mat Brook/Hebridean Whale & Dolphin Trust 6; Dundee Art Galleries and Museums 2 bottom; Laurie Campbell 14, 36, 40;
Phil Coles/Specialist Stock 24; Reinhard Dirscherl/FLPA 38; Peter Evans/Sea Watch Foundation 17, 25; Lorne Gill/SNH 1, 3, 22;
Paul Glendell/Alamy 2 top; Chris Gomersall 35 bottom; Heimir Haraar/Specialist Stock 44; Hugh Harrop front cover, 5 top, 10 bottom,
12, 21 top, 23, 29, 43; Michael Hutchinson/Specialist Stock 39; Bill Jackson 8; Charlie Phillips frontispiece, 5 bottom, 7, 30;
Charlie Phillips/Specialist Stock 35 top, 46; Todd Pusser/Naturepl 21 bottom left; Pat & Angus Macdonald 41; Hiroya Minakuchi/Minden
Pictures/FLPA 20; Flip Nicklin/Minden Pictures/FLPA 9; M. Reichelt/Sea Watch Foundation 33; Keith Ringland opposite foreword, 37;
Shetland Museum Photographic Archive opposite introduction bottom; Sea Life Surveys/Specialist Stock 27; Sue Scott opposite contents;
Peggy Stap/Nature PL 19; Tom Walmsley/Naturepl 21 bottom right; Tom Walmsley/Specialist Stock 13; Doc White/Naturepl 15.

Illustration: Ashworth Maps Interpretation Ltd 45; Martin Camm/wildlifeartcompany.com 26, 28, 31,32.

ISBN: 978 1 85397 583 7
TCP1.5K0709

Further copies are available from: Publications,
Scottish Natural Heritage, Battleby, Redgorton, Perth PH1 3EW
Tel 01738 458530 Fax 01738 456613 Email pubs@snh.gov.uk

This publication is printed on Revive Pure Silk which is 100% recycled.
This paper contains material sourced from responsibly managed and sustainable forests
certified in accordance with the FSC (Forestry Stewardship Council).

**Further booklets in this series are
available. To order these and other
publications visit: snh.org.uk/pubs**

Front cover image:
Killer whale.
Frontispiece:
Bottlenose dolphins,
mother and calf.
Back cover image:
Risso's dolphin breaching.

Whales, Dolphins & Porpoises

Naturally Scottish

by Katie Gillham and John Baxter, SNH

1

Foreword

When we think about the special wildlife of Scotland, it's easy to forget about the creatures that live offshore around our coasts. But the species inhabiting the seas are just as much part of Scotland's wildlife as those on land. Cetaceans – whales, dolphins and porpoises –are rarely seen, and poorly understood, but they are amongst the most exciting and charismatic of all the species that are 'naturally Scottish'.

It may surprise you to learn just how rich our seas are in cetaceans. Nearly one-quarter of the world's species of cetaceans are found in Scottish coastal waters. Any vessel sailing through our waters is likely to encounter these creatures regularly. Even though they may not be visible, the clicks and whistles made by porpoises and dolphins will be revealed by a hydrophone trailed behind the vessel, as the animals use echolocation to investigate their environment. To catch momentary glimpses of whales or, with good luck, to have the more prolonged company of dolphins riding the bows of a ship, is to have a brief insight into another world. Cetaceans have social structures as complex as any we know in the animal kingdom, apart from man. But these glimpses only serve to reinforce how difficult it is for us to understand what effect our presence has on these animals and why we must be cautious in our approach to their conservation.

In many ways, cetaceans are a symbol of the state of our seas. They require a 'healthy ecosystem' to support them, and are vulnerable to many man-made environmental pressures, such as chemical pollution and entanglement in fishing gear. But new issues are being presented with every new industrial and recreational development in the oceans. These include different chemicals, the rise in sound pollution, which has the potential to 'blind' these animals with high levels of background noise or with acute, high-intensity sounds, and the increasing threat of injury or death through collision with wave and tidal power generation installations. Just because we no longer actively hunt cetaceans in Scotland does not mean that we no longer have a significant effect on their populations.

The Special Area of Conservation (SAC) for bottlenose dolphins in the Moray Firth is likely to be just the start of our efforts to provide appropriate protection for cetaceans. Increased awareness, knowledge and appreciation of cetaceans at all levels of our society is the most effective route to conservation, and I welcome this book as a valuable step in that direction.

Professor Ian L Boyd
Director, Sea Mammal Research Unit,
University of St Andrews.

1
Bottlenose dolphins,
swimming off the
north-east coast.

1

Contents

1
Minke whale surfacing, between Rum and Eigg.

Off Scabra Head the lookout sighted a school
At the first light.
A meagre year it was, limpets and crows
And brief mottled grain.
Everything that could float
Circled the school. Ploughs
Wounded those wallowing lumps of thunder and night.
The women crouched and prayed.
Then whale by whale by whale
Blundering on the rock with its red stain
Crammed our winter cupboards with oil and meat.

From the The Year of the Whale
by George Mackay Brown, 1965,
and from the *Collected Poems of*
George Mackay Brown, 2005.
Reproduced by permission of the
Estate of George Mackay Brown

Introduction

Whales and Scotland

3

Scots and Scotland have a long association with whales that can be traced back to prehistory. Excavation of Stone Age settlements in the Western and Northern Isles has revealed that most parts of a dead whale were put to good use. Bones, for example, were used to make pot lids, cups, door frames and fence posts.

Until quite recent times, the accidental stranding of a large whale would have provided a valuable windfall for coastal communities, providing meat to supplement their diets, oil to help see them through harsh winters, bones for building and utensils, and hide for clothing. Perhaps they supplemented such opportunistic riches by deliberately driving whales ashore, as hunters still do in the Faroe islands with the annual pilot whale hunt (or 'grindadráp' in Faroese). Whaling from Scottish ports began around the early 1750s with sailing vessels mainly hunting in the cold northern Arctic waters. In 1859 the first custom-built steam-powered whaler 'The Tay' was used in the Dundee fleet, and this led to the Dundee fleet's supremacy in Scottish whaling until the end of the industry in the early 1900s. In less than a century the whalers had become victims of their own success, hunting some of these once common animals close to extinction.

1
Whale-bone arch on top of North Berwick Law.
2
Pilot whales (known locally as the caain whale) used to be a much more common sight in Shetland, and herds were once actively driven ashore (caa'd) and killed. The largest known caa was at Quendale in the south mainland when 1,540 animals were driven ashore. The last was at Weisdale in 1903 when 83 were killed.
3
The Maiden Stone, Drumdurno, Aberdeenshire, possibly including a carving of what is thought to be a beaked whale.

Between 1903 and 1929, records show that whalers killed 5,848 fin whales, 395 blue whales, 100 right whales, 95 sperm whales, 70 humpback whales and 26 northern bottlenose whales in the seas around Scotland. No wonder a serious decline in whale numbers followed soon after.

Whaling in the waters around the Outer Hebrides and Shetland ceased in 1929, although the Hebridean station worked again for two seasons in 1950–1951, and the legacy of the industry is still an important part of our culture. However, our relationship with these animals has changed significantly over the last century. We have gradually shifted away from extracting products from dead whales towards a growing interest in watching live whales, dolphins and porpoises in the wild.

Like humans, these magnificent animals are mammals, but they have developed a number of special adaptations for underwater life, ranging from the streamlined shapes of their bodies to the arrangement of their fins and blow holes on top of their heads. Perhaps most fascinating of all is the way in which they use sound for a range of purposes: to find food, to navigate, to seek potential mates and to maintain bonds within their social groups.

Our understanding of the ways in which whales, dolphins and porpoises use the waters around Scotland has improved dramatically in recent years, but there is still much more to discover. For example, little is known about the areas where they breed and have their calves; minke whales are one species commonly seen in Scottish waters, but nobody knows for sure where they go to give birth.

Today, around Scotland's coasts, whale-and dolphin-watching is becoming big business, but this depends on healthy populations of these fascinating creatures.

4

5

4
Whale jaw bone outside post office on North Ronaldsay, Orkney.
5
The 'Tay Whale' being auctioned on the beach at Stonehaven in 1884. The whale swam up the River Tay, presumably in search of herring and sprats which were abundant that year. It was chased out to sea by whaling ships which had been berthed at Dundee (Britain's premier whaling port) and harpooned, but evaded capture; it remained free for another week before it was found floating in the sea near Inverbervie and towed ashore at Stonehaven.
6
Humpback whale off Sumburgh Head, Shetland.

Cetaceans and the life aquatic

The earliest fossil whales (archaeoceti) date from 50–60 million years ago, having evolved from ancient land animals that returned to the sea. They are mammals, just like humans, and share many key biological features with us:

- they breathe air using lungs;
- they are warm-blooded;
- they give birth to live young; and
- they suckle these young on milk.

However, there are also many differences between us and whales. Although cetaceans still need to come up to the surface to breathe, they spend most of their life underwater, and they are highly adapted to this aquatic existence. Whilst cetaceans breathe air with lungs, their nostrils (blow holes) are on top of their heads. This design means that cetaceans have only to raise the tops of their heads out of the water in order to breathe.

Whereas most mammals have an outer layer of hair or fur to help keep them warm, almost all cetaceans are completely hairless. Instead, they rely on a layer of fat under their skin, known as blubber, to keep them warm. In dolphins and porpoises this may only be a few centimetres thick, but in larger whales it forms a layer over 20 centimetres thick. As well as providing insulation, blubber offers other benefits:

- it assists buoyancy;
- it helps to ensure a streamlined shape for swimming; and
- it acts as a reserve of food, especially when whales can't feed during migration or at their breeding grounds.

1
Common dolphin showing its streamlined shape.
2
Bottlenose dolphin breaching.

1

2

The word 'cetacean' comes from the Greek *ketos,* meaning a sea monster and *cetus,* in Latin, meaning a large sea animal. It is now applied to all whales, dolphins and porpoises, and the branch of zoology that studies these animals is called 'cetology'.

All cetaceans have horizontal tails (flukes), unlike fish whose tails are vertical (so a whale moves its tail up and down for propulsion, rather than from side to side). Their tails are very powerful, allowing them to accelerate quickly to high speeds, but are also very flexible, so they are agile and manoeuvrable when catching prey or avoiding predators. Over short distances, some dolphins can reach speeds of up to 39 kilometres per hour (24 mph). Other cetaceans are not quite so fast, but can maintain lower speeds over huge distances during their annual migrations. One migrating sei whale was recorded travelling 3,700 kilometres in just nine days – an average speed of 17 kilometres per hour, or over 10 mph.

At one time, the ancient ancestors of cetaceans had hind legs like many other mammals. However, these were gradually lost from the outside of the body to ensure a more streamlined shape for swimming. Remnants of these limbs remain inside the body as tiny bones close to the pelvis. The front limbs have been modified to form flippers. While the main propulsion comes from the tail, the flippers help with steering and stability in the water.

Flippers also have a role in regulating the temperature of cetaceans. Blood vessels run close beneath the skin of the flipper, without any insulating layer of blubber. By increasing blood flow to the flippers, cetaceans can cool themselves down as heat leaks from the blood vessels into the surrounding water. Conversely, they can limit blood flow to the flippers to minimize heat loss in colder waters. The dorsal fin on a cetacean's back helps stabilize the animal when it swims, and, like its flippers, also has a role in regulating body temperature. Its swept-back shape keeps the body streamlined.

3
Common dolphins.
4
Harbour porpoises.

How cetaceans feed

Cetaceans are divided into two groups called toothed whales and baleen whales.

The toothed whales group includes porpoises and dolphins, and whales such as killer whales, pilot whales and sperm whales, as well as the beaked whales, which are much rarer around Scotland. All of them are characterized by having teeth in their mouths (over 100 teeth in some porpoises) which they use to catch their prey – mostly fish. These teeth are roughly conical in shape, although they vary from the tusk-like teeth of sperm whales to the small spade-like teeth of the harbour porpoise.

Baleen, or whalebone, whales are toothless, but instead they have a series of horny plates, known as baleen, that hang down from the top jaw. The plates are very tough and are made out of the same material as our fingernails, a protein called keratin. Along the outer edges of the plates are coarse hairs that act as a sieve to help filter food out of the water. Baleen whales use these plates to feed on a range of prey, from small schooling fish to shrimp-like animals known as krill. Despite the small size of their prey, baleen whales, including the blue whale and the humpback whale, are some of the biggest animals in the world.

The scientific name for toothed whales is Odontocetes, from *odontos,* the Greek for tooth, while baleen whales are Mysticetes, from the Greek word *mystax,* meaning moustache.

1
Killer whale hunting along the Shetland coast with an escaping grey seal on the rocks nearby.
2
Humpback whale showing its baleen plates.

1

1

2

Birth, life and death

Whales are long-lived animals: minke whales can live for more than 40 years, sperm whales more than 65 years, and some female killer whales are thought to live to over 80 years.

Most cetaceans give birth to just a single young (called a calf). The mothers are devoted, and invest a large amount of time raising their young – in some cases up to three years.

Although the breeding cycles of cetaceans around Scotland are still not fully understood, they tend to be linked to the seasons. The smaller toothed whales, including dolphins and porpoises, do not undertake large migrations and typically give birth in the same areas where they hunt in the spring and summer, when food is most plentiful.

Baleen whales show a completely different breeding pattern. In the northern hemisphere, they feed in the cold waters of the Arctic and as far south as the waters around Scotland during the summer months before migrating south in the autumn to give birth in warmer waters, where they remain until the following spring. There is often little or no food available in these breeding grounds, so female baleen whales must rely on their stores of blubber to provide food for themselves and their calves. The males generally follow the females south and mate soon after they give birth.

All cetaceans suckle their young. The females produce milk which is very rich in fats and proteins, enabling the young to grow rapidly. In its first few months of life, a minke whale calf will increase its weight by between five and eight times – it takes a human baby several years to increase this much in weight. Even so, it may take 10 or 12 years before some whales reach maturity and begin to breed.

To compensate for their low birth rates and slow growth to maturity, most cetaceans have long lifespans. This lifecycle, however, leaves whales very vulnerable to any external factor that significantly increases death rates. For example, populations of humpback whales that were hunted around Scotland in the late 19th and early 20th centuries are only now thought to be showing signs of recovery, over a century later. This has important implications for the conservation of these animals.

1
Common dolphin with calf.
2
Killer whale mother and calf.

How cetaceans use sound

Detecting their environment

Underwater sound plays a crucial role in the life of all whales, dolphins and porpoises. Cetaceans are well adapted to detect a whole range of sounds underwater. These include sounds produced by water movement, such as rain falling on the water's surface and breaking waves (indicating the presence of storms), and of tides moving over areas of sea bed made of loose material such as gravel. They provide important clues about the state of the surrounding seas.

Humans have open ears with large lobes, which gather sound from a wide area. Cetaceans' ears are enclosed in chambers within their heads, which allows much better directional hearing because the sound is directed into the ear along specific pathways, for example, along the lower jaw. They are therefore very good at working out the direction from which a sound is coming, and thus can use this to help them navigate.

Cetaceans use sound to find out about their surroundings in two ways:

- passively, listening for sounds produced by other organisms or objects underwater, and using these sounds to detect the presence of prey or predators; and
- actively, by a process known as echolocation, in which they emit high frequency sounds themselves and listen to the returning echoes.

1
Fin whale.
2
White-beaked dolphin.

1

Communicating with their own kind

Cetaceans use sounds to communicate with one another. They use these sounds – called vocalizations – to maintain social bonds between groups, to coordinate their feeding activity, or to attract a mate.

The types of vocalizations used to maintain social bonds are enormously varied. Baleen whales produce only low-frequency groans or moans, whereas toothed whales produce a completely different range of sounds, including clicks, squeals and whistles. The low-frequency sounds produced by baleen whales can be transmitted over very long distances (i.e. thousands of miles), much further than those produced by toothed whales. This is essential for communication when individual whales are spread out through the vast oceans, and during their long migrations.

As well as clicks and whistles, bottlenose dolphins have been recorded making sounds resembling moans, trills, grunts, squeaks and creaking doors, all part of their complex system of communication.

3

The complexity of the language used to maintain bonds between individuals seems to depend on the complexity of the social group in which the animals live. Bottlenose dolphins live in groups with tight social bonds and have well-developed communication. On the other hand, minke whales tend to form much looser associations. Typically, they travel alone or in groups of two or three, although they may come together in larger numbers at feeding grounds. Their social sounds reflect this, with their vocalizations restricted to just a series of simple moans.

Vocalizations are also used to advertise a whale's presence and to find a mate. This is particularly important for cetaceans that do not live in large groups. Baleen whales mostly live a solitary life, spread out over large areas of ocean where the chances of simply encountering a potential partner are not very high, and they rely heavily on their calls to find a mate. This has become even more important as a result of hunting, which has drastically reduced their numbers and made it even more difficult for them to seek out others of their kind. Before the age of steam and more recent technological developments and military activities there was little to interfere with these long-distance communications, but the hubbub of noises that humans produce in the sea, from the likes of shipping, oil drilling, sonar systems and missile testing, now confuses their calls.

Some cetaceans also use sound to advertise that they have found food. The vocalizations of killer whales when hunting fish support a complex, cooperative system of hunting, designed to ensure that, once found, few of their prey escape.

The blue whale is one of the loudest animals on Earth – its low-frequency moans are so low that they are below the range of human hearing but have been measured at about 180–190 decibels (compared to a jumbo jet taking off at 120 decibels).

4

3
Bottlenose dolphins breaching.
4
Blue whale surfacing.

Echolocation

Echolocation is a sophisticated technique used by some cetaceans to find out more about their surroundings, in a similar way to bats. It involves them producing a sound (usually too high-pitched for humans to hear) and then listening for the corresponding echo as it bounces off nearby objects.

All toothed whales are known to echolocate, but the system used by the bottlenose dolphin is best studied and understood. When echolocating, bottlenose dolphins produce a series of very rapid clicks which are focused into a beam through its rounded forehead, known as the melon, and projected into the water in front of the animal. Each click lasts for a very short period of time (less than one thousandth of a second), and bottlenose dolphins have been recorded producing up to a thousand of these clicks in a second. The more clicks the dolphin sends out, the more information it will receive back, so as a dolphin homes in on its prey it will produce increasingly rapid clicks. The dolphin can alter the shape of its melon using muscles in the head, and this is thought to change the characteristics of the sound passing through it.

When a click hits the surface of an object, it is reflected and bounces back to the dolphin as an echo. By listening to the reflected sound, a dolphin will be able to tell not only where the object is, but also whether it is rough or smooth, hard or soft. From a series of echoes, it can tell whether and how the object is moving, and this helps it find its prey. Dolphins often sweep their heads from side to side when echolocating, allowing them to pick up as much information as possible.

It has been shown that bottlenose dolphins using echolocation can detect an object the size of a matchbox from 72 metres away.

5
Minke whale underwater.
6
Pod of long-finned pilot whales. These can be identified by their dark skin, rounded foreheads and low dorsal fins.

6

At home in the sea

Whales, dolphins and porpoises are elusive animals. Because they live most of their lives underwater, often far from the coast, it has often been simply a matter of luck when and if they are spotted at sea.

However, new technological developments using hydrophones have begun to give us a better idea of their lives at sea. Hydrophones are underwater microphones which can be used to detect noises beneath the surface, including those produced by cetaceans. They allow us to detect animals even when they are underwater, and can be used over great distances and in poor light conditions. Hydrophones can be attached to the sea bed and used to provide information about cetaceans' movements in a particular area. Alternatively, they can be used on survey ships to find out about cetacean distribution over a wide area.

Of the 23 species of cetaceans that have been recorded in Scottish waters over the last 25 years, only harbour porpoises, common and bottlenose dolphins are regularly found in both inshore and offshore waters. Pilot whales and Atlantic white-sided dolphins are common in offshore waters, but it is unusual to see them near the coast, although Atlantic white-sided dolphins are quite regularly seen in inshore waters around Scotland. Eight other species frequently occur around Scotland, although their individual distributions are quite different. For example, white-beaked dolphins occur frequently in inshore waters and offshore out to a depth of about 200 metres, whilst sperm whales are mainly found in deeper waters far offshore.

Many places that are important for cetaceans are also frequented by other marine predators, including seabirds and seals which are at the top of the food chain. At the base of these food chains are microscopic plants called phytoplankton. These thrive where there are rich supplies of nutrients in the sunlit zone near the sea's surface. The phytoplankton are eaten by a wide range of planktonic animals and larvae which in turn are fed on by fish, and seabirds move in to feed on them. Both toothed and baleen whales also exploit these abundant food supplies. Indeed, busy gatherings of feeding seabirds can sometimes be a useful indication that there may be cetaceans nearby.

In the open ocean, all that seafarers often see of whales are the spouts or blows they make when they surface. However, these may be enough to identify the species. For example, humpback whales have wide, bushy blows up to three metres tall, fin whales make much taller, columnar spouts up to six metres high, and sperm whales produce low, bushy blows that project forward at an angle.

1
A pod of Risso's dolphins.

Cetaceans frequently seen in Scottish waters

Species	Abundance estimate
Harbour porpoise *Phocoena phocoena*	385,600 in European Union waters
Bottlenose dolphin *Tursiops truncatus*	130 in the Moray Firth (1999); 650 off North East Scotland; 7,300 off West UK (2005)
Risso's dolphin *Grampus griseus*	142 individuals identified in the Minch (1999)
White-beaked dolphin *Lagenorhynchus albirostris*	10,500 in North Sea and English Channel (2005); 22,665 in North East Atlantic Shelf (2005)
Atlantic white-sided dolphin *Lagenorhynchus acutus*	74,600 off North West and West Scotland (1998); 20,000 in Faroe–Shetland Channel (2005)
Common dolphin *Delphinus delphis*	63,400 in European Union Atlantic region (2005)
Killer whale *Orcinus orca*	3,500–12,500 in eastern North Atlantic (1990)
Long-finned pilot whale *Globicephala melas*	778,000 in North Atlantic (1987/9)
Sperm whale *Physeter macrocephalus*	6010 in North East Atlantic (2002)
Fin whale *Balaenoptera physalus*	4,100 in North East Atlantic (2001); 25,800 in central North Atlantic (2001)
Minke whale *Balaenoptera acutorostrata*	10,540 in North Sea and surrounding areas (2005) 112,000 in eastern North Atlantic (1995)

1

Cetaceans sighted occasionally in Scottish waters

Species	
Striped dolphin	*Stenella coeruleoalba*
Northern bottlenose whale	*Hyperoodon ampullatus*
Cuvier's beaked whale	*Ziphius cavirostris*
Sowerby's beaked whale	*Mesoplodon bidens*
True's beaked whale	*Mesoplodon mirus*
Sei whale	*Balaenoptera borealis*
Blue whale	*Balaenoptera musculus*
Humpback whale	*Megaptera novaengliae*
Beluga whale	*Delphinapterus leucas*
Northern right whale	*Eubalaeana glacialis*
False killer whale	*Pseudorca crassidens*
Pygmy sperm whale	*Kogia breviceps*

2

2
Humpback whale breaching.
3
Striped dolphin breaching.
4
Cuvier's beaked whale. Dark grey to reddish brown in colour, it has an unique head shape with a smooth-sloping forehead.
5
Sei whale blowing.

Cetacean hotspots

1

Coastal waters

Coastal waters, around headlands and islands, and narrow channels are especially important feeding areas for cetaceans. For example, the well-mixed, highly productive waters of Yell Sound, in the north of the Shetland Islands, is an area where harbour porpoises can regularly be found foraging. Similarly, the waters of the Sea of the Hebrides to the south-west of Skye attract many species of cetaceans, including harbour porpoises, bottlenose, common, white-beaked, Atlantic white-sided and Risso's dolphins as well as killer and pilot whales. These are just a few examples of where cetaceans occur in Scotland; the map on page 45 highlights some of the other places to view cetaceans.

Fronts occur where two bodies of water meet and are another marine feature to which cetaceans are attracted. Differences between the temperature or salt content (salinity) of the waters prevents them from mixing easily. This resistance to mixing results in turbulent waters which drag nutrients from deep below up towards the surface, producing rich feeding. These fronts typically are seasonal features – they form in spring and are broken down in autumn with the first winter storms. The main fronts around Scotland are the Islay Front, the Orkney–Shetland Front and the Aberdeen Front, with smaller fronts in the outer Firths of Forth and Tay. All of these fronts are areas where cetaceans can occur in high numbers. For example, minke whales can be seen on most days in summer from the Isle of May, and close to the front in the outer Firth of Forth, and some killer whales are closely associated with seal haul-outs around pupping time.

1
Yell Sound, an important area
for cetaceans.
2
Striped dolphins surfing the waves.

2

3

4

Offshore waters

Offshore waters around Scotland support a great range of marine species. The most common cetaceans in the seas over the continental shelf are harbour porpoises, white-beaked dolphins and minke whales. Harbour porpoises and minke whales tend to travel alone or in small groups, whereas white-beaked dolphins are more usually seen in groups of up to ten.

The edge of the continental shelf runs in a north-easterly direction, from west of the Western Isles to north of the Shetland Islands. This zone, known as the shelf break, where the deep ocean meets the shallow shelf waters, is an important habitat for cetaceans. Moving out from the coast, this is the first area where deep-water species, such as sperm, pilot and beaked whales, occur more frequently, and even humpback whales may turn up occasionally.

In deeper waters offshore, the sea bed is far from featureless. Channels, ridges, seamounts (underwater mountains) and banks all occur here, affecting productivity and creating good feeding areas for cetaceans. Cold, deep Arctic waters flowing south down the Faroe–Shetland Channel are deflected by an underwater mountain chain called the Wyville–Thomson Ridge into the path of warmer waters flowing northwards. Just as with a front in coastal waters, this results in turbulence and brings more food and nutrients to the sea surface. Sperm, fin, pilot and beaked whales are typical species occurring in such areas, as well as Atlantic white-sided dolphins.

3
Northern bottlenose whales, resting in a sea loch, Isle of Skye.
4
Minke whale, lunge feeding.

Scotland's big four

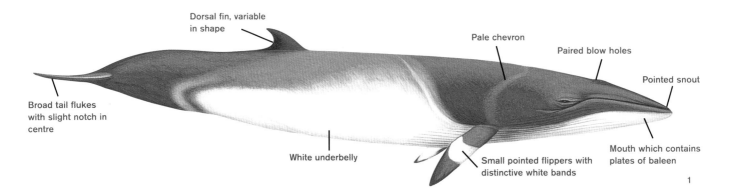

Dorsal fin, variable in shape

Pale chevron

Paired blow holes

Pointed snout

Broad tail flukes with slight notch in centre

White underbelly

Small pointed flippers with distinctive white bands

Mouth which contains plates of baleen

1

Minke whale

Minke whales are the smallest of the baleen whales, but they are still pretty big
– typically around eight or nine metres long and weighing up to nine tonnes.
They are closely related to fin, sei and blue whales. As well as being smaller
than the others, the most obvious way to tell a minke whale is to look at the
shape of its head. It is slender and streamlined with a pointed, triangular head
and a single prominent ridge running forward from the blow hole to its snout.

Minke whales feed on a wide variety of different animals, including sandeels,
herring, cod, haddock, mackerel and krill. They do not live in large groups; they
are usually found swimming individually or in pairs but can congregate in
groups of ten or more animals when a good source of food is found – up to
100 have been seen at feeding sites in Norway. This is when they are at their
most impressive: they lunge through the water on their sides, with their
enormous mouths stretched wide open to engulf a shoal of fish, erupting right
out of the water with a huge splash, then snapping their mouths shut to capture
as much food as possible.

Minke whales undertake long migrations southwards to give birth and breed,
but the locations of their breeding and calving grounds remain a mystery. Some
individuals have been found to spend whole summers feeding around the Isle of
Mull, stocking up for the long trip ahead. In the Moray Firth, some return from
their breeding grounds as early as March or April; most sightings around the
Western Isles and along the west and south-east coasts occur between May
and September. Around Orkney and Shetland they are regularly seen in August
and September.

1
Illustration of minke whale.
2
Minke whale surfacing.

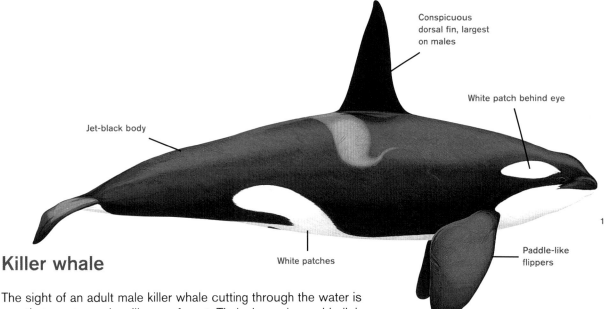

Conspicuous dorsal fin, largest on males

White patch behind eye

Jet-black body

White patches

Paddle-like flippers

1

Killer whale

The sight of an adult male killer whale cutting through the water is one that most people will never forget. Their sheer size and bulk is awe-inspiring: the largest can be up to nine metres long, with a maximum weight of 10 tonnes. Their dorsal fins can be 1.8 metres tall – around the height of an adult human. The striking black and white colouration of killer whales also means that there is little possibility of confusing them with any other cetaceans.

Killer whales are found in both shallow coastal waters and in deeper water to the north and west of Scotland. They live in organized and highly social groups known as pods. In Scottish coastal waters these groups tend to have up to eight members, but in deeper, offshore waters they may contain up to 100 animals. The oldest female is usually the dominant animal in the pod, and strong bonds are maintained between mothers and their offspring.

The value of these bonds can be seen most obviously in the way a pod of killer whales hunts. Different pods have preferences for different types of food. Some specialize in catching schooling fish, such as herring and mackerel, often in large pods; others target seals or small cetaceans, usually by hunting in smaller groups. Although some prey may be caught by individual whales, pod members work closely together to herd and eventually capture their prey. When hunting, communication between individuals, using a variety of honks and screams, is vital to ensure that they work together effectively and leave no room for prey to escape. Some killer whales have been seen playing with their food, in particular, tossing both seals and porpoises into the air, an activity which is thought to be a way of teaching their young to hunt.

The best chance of seeing killer whales in Scottish waters is when pods come closer inshore between April and September around the Western Isles, the west mainland, and the Northern Isles.

Killer whales are no more killers than any other kind of cetacean, and technically they belong to the dolphin family, so many people prefer to use the alternative name of *Orca*.

1
Illustration of killer whale.
2
Killer whales, Shetland.

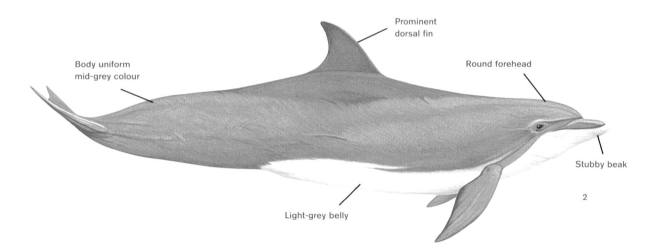

Prominent
dorsal fin

Body uniform
mid-grey colour

Round forehead

Stubby beak

2

Light-grey belly

Bottlenose dolphin

Bottlenose dolphins are perhaps the best-known cetaceans found around Scotland and can grow up to three metres in length and weigh around 200 kilograms. They occur regularly close to the shore in specific areas, and are therefore easier to see from land than other cetaceans. One population has its main base in the Moray Firth, but is actually made up of lots of small groups that spend their time ranging along the east coast of Scotland. Chanonry Point in the Moray Firth is an excellent spot for watching them.

Their diet is very diverse and includes flatfish, herring, mackerel, cod and salmon, squid and octopus, and different types of shellfish. Their behaviour is also varied. They can be seen somersaulting, breaching sideways out of the water and performing tail slaps – perhaps why this species is the commonest dolphin kept in captivity in dolphinaria. Like some other species of dolphins, they will often actively swim towards boats to ride in the bow-waves.

However, what we see at the surface is only part of the picture. Like killer whales, bottlenose dolphins live in social groups and take part in cooperative hunting. In the Moray Firth, bottlenose dolphins are also known to kill harbour porpoises, although the reasons for this behaviour are not fully understood.

In coastal waters, groups can include up to as many as 25 animals. This may have led to the development of a whole range of social behaviour not known in other species. Their ability to use sound to communicate is also highly developed. There is increasing evidence that each dolphin has its own distinctive whistle, like a unique signature tune.

1
Bottlenose dolphins providing an acrobatic display.
2
Illustration of bottlenose dolphin.

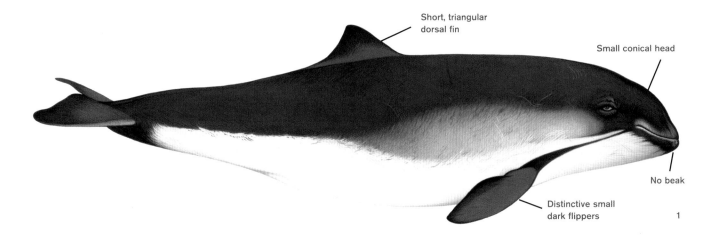

Short, triangular dorsal fin

Small conical head

No beak

Distinctive small dark flippers

1

Harbour porpoise

Harbour porpoises are the smallest cetaceans found in Scottish waters. They are just 1.35–1.8 metres long, and weigh up to 90 kg. They have small, rounded bodies and short heads, without the typical beaks of dolphins. Although closely related to dolphins, there are a number of differences between them. To anyone watching from the surface, the easiest way to distinguish them is to look at the shape of the dorsal fin on the animal's back. All the dolphins found in Scottish waters have tall, sickle-shaped dorsal fins, whereas the fin of the harbour porpoise is small and triangular in shape.

Harbour porpoises are the most abundant cetaceans found in Scottish coastal waters. They are typically found in shallow, coastal waters with depths of less than about 100 metres. Although they are found throughout Scottish waters, they are more common along the west coast and around the Western and Northern Isles, particularly in summer. If you are patient and watch carefully from a headland in these areas, there is a good chance you may see a harbour porpoise, although, in rough weather, it can be difficult to pick out their small dorsal fins in choppy waters.

Harbour porpoises feed on a wide range of fish, including herring, whiting and sandeels. They usually travel alone or in small groups. However, if they find an abundant source of food, they will often come together to feed in groups of 100 animals or more, creating a spectacular sight. They are much less likely to display than other cetaceans. Most typically, you will get only a glimpse of a porpoise passing by quickly, coming occasionally to the surface to breathe, as it moves on to other feeding areas.

Porpoises belong to a family of small toothed whales, called the Phocoenidae. There are just six species, and only the harbour porpoise is found around Scotland. The main distinguishing feature from dolphins is that they have flattened teeth.

1
Illustration of harbour porpoise.
2
Harbour porpoise surfacing to breathe.

2

Threats to cetaceans

Entanglement in fishing gear

The accidental capture of cetaceans in fishing nets is called bycatch. This becomes a problem when cetaceans and fishermen regularly use the same areas of sea at the same time, both trying to find the best places to catch fish. The interaction between fisheries and cetaceans can result in negative impacts on both. Cetaceans may become entangled in fishing gear, resulting in injury or drowning. This is bad news for the fishermen too, because their gear may be damaged in the process, resulting in lost earnings and additional costs for replacing broken equipment.

In Scottish waters, harbour porpoises are the species most susceptible to being caught in fishing nets. Nets set on the sea bed have the highest levels of bycatch, because this is where porpoises tend to feed most. It is estimated that around 400 harbour porpoises die in the North Sea each year as a result of being caught in fishing gear.

Under a variety of legislation, conventions and agreements – including the EU Habitats Directive and the Agreement on Small Cetaceans of the Baltic and North Sea (ASCOBANS) – Scotland is committed to take action to avoid or reduce the level of cetacean bycatch. To meet this commitment, the UK Small Cetacean Bycatch Response Strategy has been developed, this sets out measures to address the problem, including the use of acoustic deterrents, called pingers, better monitoring of populations and bycatch, and an accreditation scheme for cetacean-friendly fisheries.

Loss of food supplies

The waters around Scotland are intensively fished for a wide range of species, many of which are also important food for cetaceans. Overfishing of herring, mackerel and other species could have significant impacts on cetacean populations. Over the last 50 years herring stocks have been severely depleted, and numbers of harbour porpoises have declined greatly over the same period. Evidence of the link between these two species was shown in 1977, when a fishing ban resulted in a partial recovery of herring stocks. This was followed by a slight increase in the number of sightings of harbour porpoises. The decline in abundance of sandeels has also had an effect on cetacean numbers as well as seabirds and other predators.

The harbour porpoise and minke whale are both so fond of herring that in places they are known as the herring hog.

1
Bottlenose dolphins
bow-riding a fishing boat,
Cromarty Firth.
2
Harbour porpoises in Loch
Nevis - on calm days listen out
for the sound that porpoises
make as they surface to
breathe. The distinctive short
puff has led to them being
known in Shetland as neesiks,
the local word for a sneeze.

1

2

Chemical pollution

Various chemicals are released either directly or indirectly into coastal waters. Sources of these contaminants include effluent from industry along our coasts, domestic sewage, anti-fouling paints used on ships and other man-made structures, and pesticides. Of particular concern are chemicals such as organochlorines that accumulate in animals' bodies and are then passed up through the food chain to top predators, including cetaceans. Some of these chemicals have been associated with impaired immune systems and reduced rates of reproduction in cetaceans. Although the manufacture of organochlorines is now strictly controlled in Scotland, these chemicals break down very slowly in the marine environment, so, unfortunately, they will continue to affect cetaceans and other species for a long time to come.

3

3
Sperm whale vertebra.
4
Bottlenose dolphin breaching with platform supply vessel in the distance.

Noise pollution

Until the late 19th century, sailing boats were the main form of sea travel. These have now been largely replaced by ships driven by engines, which often sound especially noisy underwater. More recently, the use of sonar, drilling and other activities relating to oil and gas exploration, military training at sea, and the use of acoustic seal deterrents at fish farms have also greatly increased this underwater noise.

There is evidence that some types of underwater noises damage individual cetaceans. More commonly they drown out naturally occurring sounds which are an important source of biological information for cetaceans. With so much human-generated noise around, they may have problems locating their food, and may be unable to detect the sound of approaching predators or potential mates.

Sonar, used in ship navigation, interferes with naturally occurring sounds. Most sonar produces pulses of mid-frequency sound that overlaps with the hearing ranges of toothed whales. In some parts of the world it is thought that naval exercises using sonar might have caused damage to the hearing of cetaceans, resulting in behavioural changes and, in some cases, to mass strandings. New 'active sonar' systems are being developed that operate at much lower frequencies. These overlap with frequencies used by baleen whales, and send out more powerful sound pulses over much longer distances.

4

Cetacean conservation

Action for biodiversity

Biodiversity Action Plans (BAPs) are the response of the UK Government and Scottish Ministers to the Convention on Biological Diversity, developed at the 'Earth Summit' in Rio de Janeiro in 1992. In Scotland, a Marine and Coastal Ecosystem Delivery Plan sets out a series of actions aimed at ensuring that the seas around Scotland are managed more sustainably. The Plan is renewed every three years. Under the UK BAP, 20 species of cetaceans were identified as marine priority species in 2007. Work is now underway to determine which actions are a priority for cetaceans found in Scottish waters.

Some cetaceans are also the subject of local Biodiversity Action Plans (LBAPs), which identify conservation actions at a local level. LBAP actions vary from more general work, in promoting the importance of an area for cetaceans, through to more specific tasks. For example, people may want to carry out a survey of cetaceans using a particular area so that they can ensure that effective management is put in place to help in their conservation.

1

All of this work will in future be supported by the EU Marine Strategy Framework Directive which aims to ensure good environmental conditions across European seas for all the species that live there. The status of cetacean populations is one of the ways in which the condition of our seas will be assessed. Different countries will be expected to work together to put appropriate management in place. This is good news, particularly for cetaceans, who may travel great distances between the waters of a number of countries.

Legal protection

Two different approaches are being taken to the conservation of cetaceans in Scottish waters:

– identifying small, defined areas that are particularly important for cetaceans and managing activities likely to affect these sites; and
– identifying activities that occur throughout Scottish waters that have an impact on cetacean populations, then establishing ways to carry out those activities so that impacts are minimized.

Both approaches can be enhanced and encouraged by appropriate legislation.

All cetaceans have full legal protection under the EU Habitats Directive (which has also been transposed into Scots law). This aims to better protect all cetaceans and their habitats, and means that they must be given special consideration by anyone who is planning to carry out activities that might have an impact on their lives.

The Habitats Directive also singles out two species for special consideration: the bottlenose dolphin and the harbour porpoise. Both of these are listed on Annex II of the Directive, which requires that sites which are essential for the survival of these species should be designated and protected as Special Areas of Conservation (SACs). The Moray Firth has been identified as an SAC for bottlenose dolphins in Scotland.

Furthermore, the Nature Conservation (Scotland) Act makes it an offence to disturb deliberately or recklessly or to harass any cetaceans. Further details of the legal protection offered to cetaceans by European and Scottish legislation can be found in the revised edition of *Scotland's wildlife: The law and you.*

1
Sperm whale.
2
Hebridean Whale and Dolphin Trust research survey ship, the 'Silurian'. Researchers are towing a blue hydrophone cable to monitor sounds made by cetaceans.

3

Site protection: the Moray Firth Special Area of Conservation

The Moray Firth Special Area of Conservation (SAC) covers an area of 1,513 km^2 and is home to the most northerly population of bottlenose dolphins in the world. The population consists of about 130 animals which spend the majority of the year in and around the Moray Firth, although some are known to travel as far south as Berwick-upon-Tweed on occasions.

The Moray Firth Partnership and the Moray Firth SAC Management Group have led the process of developing a management scheme for the bottlenose dolphins (as well as for the sandbanks, which are another important feature of the site). The management challenges facing the Moray Firth partnership and the Moray Firth SAC Management Group have been:

– raising awareness about the impact of illegal salmon netting on bottlenose dolphins and other marine wildlife;
– highlighting the SAC and promoting adherence to codes of practice to minimize disturbance by boat traffic, including mention on the latest version of the Inverness Firth Admiralty Chart; and
– production of a review of the effects of environmental contaminants on bottlenose dolphins, also considering water quality standards for dolphins.

The scheme contains many actions that aim to benefit the dolphins and guide those who live and work in the area to carry out their activities in a manner that reflects the special interests of the site. The scheme can be viewed on the Moray Firth Partnership website (www.morayfirth-partnership.org)

3
Bottlenose dolphins at the Moray Firth demonstrating their acrobatic skills in synchronized breaching.
4
Kessock Bridge, Moray Firth.

4

Management in the wider marine environment

The development of the UK Small Cetacean Bycatch Response Strategy is an example of an approach that tackles one issue over a much wider area. The aim of the strategy is to take action not only in Scottish waters, but in all waters around the UK. This wider approach to tackling the problems of bycatch is essential because most cetaceans don't just live in the waters around Scotland, but range over much larger areas.

There are two main ways in which action can be taken to address bycatch:

– implementation of fisheries management measures (e.g. using closed areas or closed seasons to minimize the impact of fisheries in areas that are especially important for cetaceans, at least at the time of year when cetaceans gather there); and
– changes to fishing gear to minimize the risk of catching cetaceans.

An example of the latter is the use of acoustic pingers on nets set to catch fish on the sea bed, where harbour porpoises and other species hunt. These are small devices which can be attached to fishing nets. They produce a sound that discourages cetaceans from coming close to the nets. This has the double advantage of preventing damage to cetaceans by the nets and damage to the nets by cetaceans, so acoustic pingers potentially could work to everyone's advantage.

5
Watching killer whales from the shore, Shetland.

Whale watching – and how you can help

The whaling industry of the 18th and 19th centuries collapsed as first one then another species of whale were hunted almost to extinction. Now there is growing interest from people wanting to watch live whales, dolphins and porpoises in their natural environment. Thanks to this, people in Scotland are once again making a living from cetaceans – but in a much more sustainable way.

There are many headlands around the coast which offer great vantage points to sit and look out for cetaceans. However, more and more businesses are also setting up, offering boat trips to watch these animals up close. Some boats have hydrophones so you can hear the sounds that the cetaceans make underwater, and even cameras in mini-submarines that transmit underwater images back to the surface.

Whale watching is a growing eco-tourism industry, but that's not its only value. Observations and sound recordings made from the coast or from whale watching boats can make a valuable contribution to our understanding of cetacean behaviour. Although research work is carried out from dedicated ships, these can cover only a fraction of the waters around Scotland. Some skippers on whale watching boats regularly contribute records of the cetaceans that they see to organizations such as the Hebridean Whale and Dolphin Trust or The Sea Watch Foundation.

You can also help by sending in records of any whales, dolphins and porpoises that you see around Scotland. If you know of a local group that is collecting sightings you can send your cetacean records to them or, if not, send them to The Sea Watch Foundation (see Useful addresses on page 48). It's also useful to know about stranded cetaceans so that we can learn more about potential threats to these animals. If you come across a stranded whale, dolphin or porpoise, whether it is dead or alive, contact the Scottish Agricultural College (also in Useful addresses). All records are welcome and, by helping to understand more about the distribution and movements of these animals and some of the issues they face, your sightings could also help to define priorities for future conservation action.

1

1
Watching a minke whale from
a whale watching boat.

Where to see cetaceans around the Scottish coastline

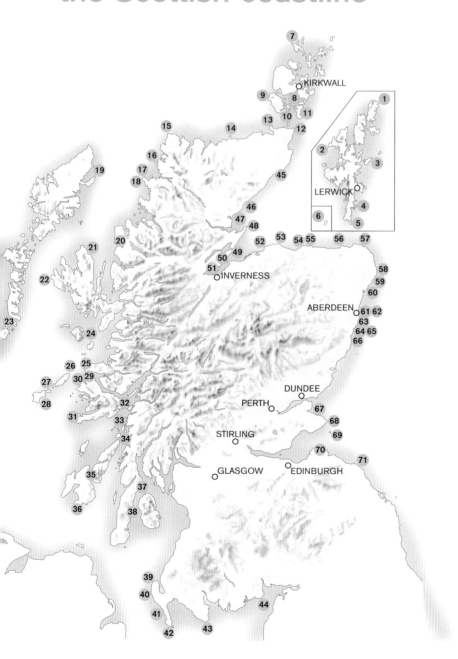

1	Lamba Ness	37	Skipness
2	Esha Ness	38	Carradale
3	Whalsay	39	Corsewall Point
4	Mousa Sound	40	Black Head
5	Sumburgh Head	41	Ardwell Point
6	Fair Isle	42	Mull of Galloway
7	Rackwick	43	Burrow Head
8	Scapa Flow	44	Southerness Point
9	Old Man of Hoy	45	Lybster
10	Cantick Head	46	Brora
11	South Ronaldsay	47	Golspie
12	Duncansby Head	48	Tarbat Ness
13	Dunnet Head	49	Sutors of Cromarty
14	Strathy Point	50	Chanonry Point
15	Cape Wrath	51	North Kessock
16	Handa Island	52	Burghead
17	Point of Stoer	53	Lossiemouth
18	Stoer Head	54	Findochty
19	Tiumpan Head	55	Cullen Bay
20	Gairloch	56	Troup Head
21	Staffin	57	Kinnaird Head
22	Neist Point	58	Peterhead
23	Sound of Barra	59	Bullers of Buchan
24	Small Isles	60	Collieston
25	Ardnamurchan Point	61	Torry Battery
26	Cairns of Coll	62	Souter Head
27	Gunna Sound	63	Cove
28	Hynish	64	Portlethen
29	Ardmore Point	65	Downies
30	Calliach Point	66	Stonehaven
31	Sound of Iona	67	St Andrews
32	Duart Point	68	Fife Ness
33	Isle of Seil	69	Isle of May
34	Craignish Point	70	North Berwick
35	Sound of Islay	71	St Abbs Head
36	Oa		

The Scottish Marine Wildlife Watching Code

Watching marine wildlife around the coast of Scotland can be a fantastic experience. In many cases, the disturbance caused by watching is minor or insignificant. With an increasing number of people involved in wildlife watching, concerns were raised about the potential impacts on our marine wildlife. In response to these concerns, Scottish Natural Heritage has developed the Scottish Marine Wildlife Watching Code. The aim of the Code is to minimize disturbance to marine wildlife, including whales, dolphins and porpoises and to make sure that watching wildlife is a good experience both for people and wildlife. The Code is accompanied by a Guide to Best Practice for Watching Marine Wildlife which contains more detailed information. Some of the recommended actions for watching cetaceans include:

– avoiding cetaceans with young;
– maintaining a slow, steady speed so that cetaceans can predict where the boat is going and therefore avoid collisions; and
– ensuring a clear escape route for cetaceans at all times.

Some operators have developed their own stricter codes, to take account of important issues in their local area. If you go on a whale watching boat trip, check before you book to make sure that the operator is following an agreed code of conduct. Adherence to these codes is essential if whale watching is to continue and develop as a sustainable industry around the coast of Scotland. By going on a whale watching trip with one of these operators, you are therefore helping this industry to develop – and showing that living whales offer far more value to the economy of coastal communities than dead ones.

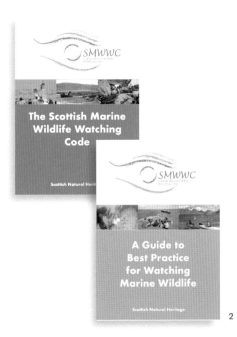

2

2
Scottish Marine Wildlife Watching Code.
3
Dolphin watching in the Moray Firth.

3

Whale, dolphin and porpoise names

Scottish name

Baffert, baffert whale, porpoise.

Blover, from Buchan, porpoise.

Bucker, from Argyll, a whale or porpoise.

Ca, 'caain' whale, from Orkney and Shetland, pilot whale.

Chaffer, from Orkney and Shetland, 'round-lipped whale'.

Delphyn fysch, dolphin.

Dunter, from Orkney for harbour porpoise or dolphin. Compare with the Norwegian word 'dynta', which means to move with a bobbing motion.

Finner, chiefly Shetland for a rorqual whale (genus *Balaenoptera*)

Flaked whale, from Orkney, white-sided dolphin.

Fleckit whale, killer whale, from fleck – to develop white patches on the skin.

Gairfish, from Dundee, dolphin or porpoise, minke whale.

Herring hog, harbour porpoise or minke whale.

Huddo(u)n, whale.

Looper dog, from Shetland, Atlantic white-sided dolphin or white-beaked dolphin.

Meer-swine, meerswine, mereswyne, dolphin or porpoise.

Mink, mynk, minke whale.

Neesiks, neesick, from Shetland, porpoise – from the Old Norse word for a sneeze.

Pellock, pellok, pallack, pallo, paalo, from Orkney, porpoise.

Puff, puffie, puffy dunter, porpoise, because of the noise that they make when surfacing.

Sea-swine, porpoise.

Stink, stynk, from Buchan, white-sided dolphin.

Stourfish, whale.

Tymbrell, porpoise.

Whaal, whaul, whale.

Gaelic name

Muc-bhiorach, bottlenose dolphin.

Deilf, common dolphin.

Deilf-risso, Risso's dolphin.

Mada-chuain, killer whale.

Muc-mhara-mhionc, minke whale.

Muc-an-Scadain, fin whale.

Muc-mhara-Sei, sei whale (muc is Gaelic for pig or sow, 'mhara' or 'mara' is Gaelic for sea or ocean).

Stair, from 'Stair(ean)' meaning stepping stones, from the similarity in appearance to a school of porpoises.

Gaelic Place Names

Eilean a Muic, Isle of Muck, the Gaelic translates as 'the island of the dolphin'.

Cana, Canna, the Gaelic 'Cana' means porpoise or young whale.

Finding out more

Further reading

Carwardine, M. 1995. *Eyewitness Handbooks: Whales, Dolphins and Porpoises.* Dorling Kindersley.

DEFRA. 2003. *UK Small Cetacean Bycatch Response Strategy.*

Evans, P.G.H. 1995. *Guide to Identification of Whales, Dolphins and Porpoises in European Seas.* Sea Watch Foundation, Oxford.

Evans, P. & Raga, J.A. (eds). 2001. *Marine Mammals: Biology and Conservation.* Plenum Publishers.

Hoyt, E. 2004. *Marine Protected Areas for Whales, Dolphins and Porpoises: A World Handbook for Cetacean Habitat Conservation.* Earthscan Publications.

Moray Firth SAC Management Group. 2002. *Moray Firth SAC Management Scheme.*

Reid, J.B., Evans, P.G.H. & Northridge, S.P. 2003. *Atlas of Cetacean Distribution in North-West European waters.* JNCC.

Waller, G. (ed.). 1996. *Sealife: A Guide to the Marine Environment.* Christopher Helm.

Wilson, B, & Wilson, A. 2006. *The Complete Whale Watching Handbook: A Guide to Whales, Dolphins, and Porpoises of the World.* Voyageur Press.

Useful addresses

Hebridean Whale and Dolphin Trust, 28 Main Street, Tobermory, Isle of Mull, Argyll, PA75 6NU
Tel: 01688 302620
e-mail: education@hwdt.org
www.whaledolphintrust.co.uk

JNCC Seabirds and Cetaceans Branch, Dunnet House, 7 Thistle Place, Aberdeen, AB10 1UZ
Tel: 01224 655704
(from January 2010) Inverdee House, Balnagask Road, Torry, Aberdeen
www.jncc.gov.uk

Scottish Agricultural College, King's Buildings, West Mains Road, Edinburgh, EH9 3JG
Tel: 0131 535 4000
www.sac.ac.uk

Scottish Natural Heritage, Great Glen House, Leachkin Road, Inverness, IV3 8NW
Tel: 01463 725000
www.snh.org.uk

Sea Mammal Research Unit, Gatty Marine Laboratory, University of St Andrews, St Andrews, KY16 8LB
Tel: 01334 462630
www.smub.st-and.ac.uk

The Sea Watch Foundation, 11 Jersey Road, Oxford, 0X4 4RT Tel: 01865 717276
e-mail: info@seawatchfoundation.co.uk
www.seawatchfoundation.org.uk

The Whale and Dolphin Conservation Society, Brookfield House, 38 St Paul Street, Chippenham, Wiltshire, SN15 1LJ Tel: 0870 870 5001
e-mail: info@wdcs.org
www.wdcs.org

Wild Scotland, Thistle House, Beechwood Park North, Inverness, IV2 3ED Tel: 01463 723013
www.wild-scotland.org.uk